GUIDE TO THE THUNDER SWAMP TRAIL

SECOND EDITION

BEN CRAMER

CATAMOUNT
PRESS

an imprint of Sunbury Press, Inc.
Mechanicsburg, PA USA

CATAMOUNT
PRESS

an imprint of Sunbury Press, Inc.
Mechanicsburg, PA USA

For information about special discounts for bulk purchases, please contact Sunbury Press Orders Dept. at (855) 338-8359 or orders@sunburypress.com.

To request one of our authors for speaking engagements or book signings, please contact Sunbury Press Publicity Dept. at publicity@sunburypress.com.

FIRST CATAMOUNT PRESS EDITION: October 2025

Set in Adobe Garamond | Interior design by Crystal Devine | Cover by Lawrence Knorr | Edited by Debra Reynolds. All photos by the author.

Publisher's Cataloging-in-Publication Data
Names: Cramer, Ben, author.
Title: Guide to the Thunder Swamp Trail / Ben Cramer.
Description: First trade paperback edition. | Mechanicsburg, PA : Catamount Press, 2025.
Summary: A point-by-point guide to the Thunder Swamp Trail and its Northeast Spur, which form a 32-mile hiking network in Pike County, Pennsylvania that travels through Delaware State Forest and Stillwater Natural Area.
Identifiers: ISBN : 979-8-88819-353-2 (softcover).
Subjects: SPORTS & RECREATION / Hiking | TRAVEL / Northeast / Middle Atlantic (NJ, NJ, PA) | NATURE / Regional.

Designed in the USA
0 1 1 2 3 5 8 13 21 34 55

For the Love of Books!

Cover: A swamp at the origin of Spruce Run, as seen from the northwestern section of the Thunder Swamp Trail.

TABLE OF CONTENTS

AUTHOR'S NOTE

This trail guide accurately reflects measurements and observations that were made along the Thunder Swamp Trail during an inspection by the author in Spring 2024. Original measurements taken for the previous edition of this guidebook in 2021 have been re-checked for accuracy. All efforts have been made to ensure accuracy in descriptions of the features and logistics of the trail and the distances involved. However, conditions in the natural world are constantly changing. Fallen trees, flash floods, forestry practices, human developments, and myriad other phenomena often necessitate the rerouting of hiking trails and can damage infrastructure such as footbridges. Changes in the route or condition of the trail may be completed by the Pennsylvania Department of Conservation and Natural Resources, Keystone Trails Association, or other volunteers after this guide is published.

All persons using this guide do so at their own risk, and this guide should not be used without adequate maps and other common-sense precautions, which should be practiced by all outdoorspersons. The author, publisher, and all trail workers/volunteers disclaim any and all liability for trail conditions, hazards, incidents encountered by hikers, and inaccuracies in this guide that may be the result of future developments. Also, the reader should follow this guide's recommendations for water sources and camping locations at his or her own risk. Please contact the author about any changes encountered along the trail that should be included in future editions of this guide.

ACKNOWLEDGMENTS

The joy of hiking in Pennsylvania would not be possible without the contributions of volunteer trail builders, maintainers, and observers. Hikers and backpackers may not even notice the valuable work of these volunteers, but they would surely notice if all that hard work was no longer being performed. Thanks to all the trail club volunteers and state forest employees in Pennsylvania who make our trails so enjoyable.

Special thanks to Brook Lenker of Keystone Trails Association for providing a connection with Sunbury Press, where Lawrence Knorr and his team have been instrumental in getting this book into your hands.

Ben Cramer, June 2025

ABOUT THE THUNDER SWAMP TRAIL

INTRODUCTION

The Thunder Swamp Trail (TST) traverses a segment of Delaware State Forest in southern Pike County in the Pocono Mountains region of northeastern Pennsylvania. The trail is found about halfway between Interstates 80 and 84 and is reached from either of those via Pennsylvania Route 402. It is also within easy reach of the city of Stroudsburg, which is about 15 miles to the south.

Stroudsburg is a convenient spot for obtaining supplies, with a full range of stores and restaurants. As the gateway to the Pocono Mountains and a magnet for tourists from throughout the Northeast, the city offers plentiful hotels in every conceivable price range, from threadbare roadside motels to touristy mega-resorts. There are also several organized campgrounds in the area. To the north, there are convenient stores and occasional hotels at various exit ramps off I-84.

There are actually two trails in the Thunder Swamp Trail system: a "Main Loop" of **18.28 miles** that is roughly bisected by PA 402; and an extension trail branching off the Main Loop that can be hiked in both directions for a total of **13.39 miles**. The extension trail is usually described in conjunction with the Main Loop but with no official name of its own; it is sometimes called the Painter Swamp Trail informally though that name does not appear on recent state forest maps. The present author has decided to call it the "Northeast Spur" to prevent confusion. Each is described in its own chapter later in this book.

The Northeast Spur, as its new informal name implies, departs from the Main Loop and heads northeast toward a Natural Area in a remote corner of Delaware State Forest. It is also what some hikers call a "lollipop" trail because it has a two-way section and a mini-loop. At its furthest extremity, the Northeast Spur leads to its own mini-loop at Big Bear

Swamp, which the hiker can go around in one direction and then return on the two-way portion of the Northeast Spur, back to the TST's Main Loop to the southwest.

As a system of trails, the TST is often described as **25.6 miles** in length or thereabouts, including in the most recent map published by Delaware State Forest. This includes the Main Loop plus the Northeast Spur, if you hiked that spur in only one direction. This is nonsensical for the long-distance hiker's planning purposes, because after 25.6 miles you would be stranded at the far end of the Northeast Spur and would find that the State Forest did not tell you that you must hike the Northeast Spur again in the other direction to return to your starting point. There are also some older books and websites that describe the Thunder Swamp Trail as 40 to 45 miles in length, but that figure included many spur trails that have since been differentiated from the Main Loop and Northeast Spur with differently colored blazes.

If you start at the official trailhead at the southern end of the Main Loop, walk around that loop to the junction with the Northeast Spur, complete that spur *in both directions* and return to the junction with the Main Loop, and then complete the Main Loop back to your starting point, the result would be a grand total of **31.67 miles**.

The TST encounters some Natural Areas within Delaware State Forest, where there are tougher controls on logging and other developments. Along the western section of the Main Loop there is a junction with a short side trail that leads to Pennel Run Natural Area (with further trails under development as of 2025), while the Northeast Spur directly visits Stillwater Natural Area.

These Natural Areas highlight the state's noble efforts at preservation, but a quick glance at the state forest map shows that the Natural Areas (and Delaware State Forest itself) are severely fragmented and gerrymandered to avoid the private landholdings that are speckled across the Pocono region. Those are often used for luxury resorts and vacation homes, meaning that the protected tracts have been pried from developers (or have been deemed undesirable by developers) and do not necessarily correspond with ecosystems and other natural features.

This area of Delaware State Forest also contains about 15 additional miles of developed trails. Those are only mentioned briefly in this guide, but they are visible on State Forest maps and can be used for creative loop hikes or shortcuts back to your starting point.

HISTORY AND CHARACTERISTICS

Information on the history of the Thunder Swamp Trail and its inspirations is scant and tough to obtain. Present personnel at Delaware State Forest seem to have lost any such information beyond the basic, if anything further was ever recorded. What we do know is that the trail was built in the 1970s by the Youth Conservation Corps (YCC), which in turn was a federal program to provide outdoor-oriented work and experience for teenagers.

The inspiration for this particular trail construction project seems to be unrecorded, though it was probably like that for other projects in the State Forests of the region, with the goal of providing rugged outdoor opportunities and access to remote points of interest. This was the documented inspiration for the Pinchot Trail System in the State Forest of that name about 30 miles to the west, where more information is available about passionate local volunteers who suggested routes and helped with scouting and construction.

Longtime Pennsylvania hiking authority Tom Thwaites (1931-2014) dug up some information on the history of the Thunder Swamp Trail for his 1997 book *50 Hikes in Eastern Pennsylvania*. According to Thwaites, despite the many swamps visited by the trail, there was no actual "Thunder Swamp" in the area and the YCC workers simply made up the name for the trail because it sounded cool. However, the current official map for Delaware State Forest features a place called Thunder Swamp, near the village of Ludleyville, so perhaps life imitates art.

The area traversed by the TST system indeed features many swamps and wetlands, but only some of them are visible from the trail. This is because if a hiking trail got too close to a swamp, the landscape would be too soggy and this in turn would require prohibitively expensive boardwalks, drainage systems, causeways, bridges, and the like. Therefore, the hiker on the Thunder Swamp Trail will note open areas through the trees in the distance, where most of the swamps are really found. The adventurous outdoorsperson will find more natural wonders with some off-trail exploration but should expect wet feet and dense vegetation in the process.

BLAZES AND TRAIL SIGNS

The TST's Main Loop and Northeast Spur are both marked with rectangular orange blazes as officially designated Pennsylvania state forest trails. These are painted on trees and are usually visible from a comfortable distance, except for a few challenging areas that are described in this guide. Blazes may occasionally be found on rocks underfoot. Turns are usually denoted by double blazes and sometimes arrows.

The network also includes fairly frequent wooden signs denoting the distance to points of interest ahead. However, for the reasons stated above concerning trail construction in swampy areas, the trail does not truly reach some of the locations denoted on the signs. For example, signs on the eastern portions of the Main Loop say that Lake Minisink is a certain distance ahead, but you only see that lake very dimly through the trees when you reach that area. That is just one example among several.

This area of Delaware State Forest includes several other trails that connect to the TST; those are usually marked with yellow blazes. Those trails are not described in detail in this guidebook, but they are worth exploring in their own right during extended trips to the area. Most such trails are visible on maps published by Delaware State Forest, and hikers who are good at estimating distances can use those for creative hikes in conjunction with the TST.

THE HIKING LANDSCAPE

The Thunder Swamp Trail system sits on top of a relatively flat plateau in southern Pike County. Of course, this region is part of the famous "Pocono Mountains," but the Poconos are not really a mountain range and are better described as a plateau that rises in steps above the Delaware River from the east. From the viewpoint of a tiny human on the ground, the plateau may look mountainous because it is dented by creek valleys and supplemented by sporadic hills and ridges at the high points.

The Thunder Swamp Trail system encounters no significant climbs. There is a fair amount of elevation gain but it tends to happen over long distances, as the landscape gradually rises or falls underfoot. On some parts of the trail, you will also encounter an irregular "staircase" landscape of flat rock slabs; in other words, you walk across generally flat ground for a long period, abruptly scramble up or down a short ridgeline, and then continue across another flat area.

If you circuit-hike the TST Main Loop, your total elevation gain will be about 2,100 feet, which is not very dramatic for 18.28 miles. The TST Northeast Spur, when completed in both directions, adds about 1,100 feet of elevation gain.

The highest point in the network is at about 1,430 feet in elevation, on the Northeast Spur a little east of Bushkill Falls Road. The lowest point in the network is on the Main Loop at the confluence of Red Rock Run and Saw Creek, at about 930 feet, while there is another low point of about 950 feet at the trail's first encounter with Bushkill Creek. Those two low points are outliers because most of the trail system stays relatively flat between about 1,100 and 1,300 feet of elevation.

However, don't be lulled into complacency by the Thunder Swamp Trail's relatively flat route. As a longtime and experienced hiker, I have found the TST to be one of the *slowest* trails I have ever traversed, in terms of hiking miles per hour. This is because of the excessively rocky landscape, with miles and miles of sharp jagged rocks underfoot for most of the trail system. Be prepared for slow progress, aching joints, and possibly even injuries due to tripping hazards and ankle-busting angles.

The Pocono region was heavily roughed up by glaciers during the last ice age. The glaciers scoured the landscape down to the bedrock, then made the future hiker's life even harder by smashing that bedrock into jagged chunks. This endless pile of pointy rocks now has just a thin layer of topsoil to support the forest.

In many places along the TST, especially along the Northeast Spur, you walk through areas with nearly continuous tree roots underfoot, indicating that the thin soil and rocky underbed prevent the roots from sinking deep into the ground. Instead, they spread out horizontally and

A fallen tree found along the TST Northeast Spur in 2024. Note the nearly horizontal root system as the roots were unable to sink into the rocky bed just below the topsoil.

tangle amongst each other. Fallen trees show very shallow and horizontal roots, as opposed to the "rootball" effect seen with their brethren that established deep roots when they were still standing.

Meanwhile, the glaciers gouged out shallow depressions and left behind piles of rubble that blocked previous drainage patterns. This resulted in a plethora of small lakes after the glaciers retreated, many of which have filled with silt and evolved into swamps and wetlands over the millennia. This makes the Thunder Swamp Trail both rocky and swampy, often at the same time.

The rocky and swampy landscape has resisted human developments in this general area of southern Pike County. Compared to other long-distance Pennsylvania backpacking trails, the TST encounters relatively few human developments, which is especially noteworthy because there are lots of small towns and housing developments not too far away.

WILDLIFE

The aforementioned rugged landscape has resisted humans but has created a haven for wildlife. The typical Pennsylvania animals like deer, rabbits, porcupines, and groundhogs are plentiful in the area. I have heard reports of coyotes in the area but have not yet seen any. On the other hand, I have seen and/or heard many large birds along the TST, including owls, wild turkeys, and several species of hawks.

The swamp ecosystem is clearly a boon to amphibians as I have witnessed several frog and salamander species along the TST, and you are highly likely to see the common red eft (a small orange newt that favors damp areas) while hiking. On a previous trip to survey the TST, I saw *dozens* of red efts sitting on moist soil and even in shallow puddles on Snow Hill Road. Keep an eye out for these tiny but noticeably orange creatures underfoot; they are not very fast and are likely to be stepped on.

Bears and rattlesnakes are also prevalent in the region; I have seen both along the TST. In 2019, I saw an eastern timber rattlesnake along the Northeast Spur near Painter Swamp, and later that year I saw two

A red eft spotted on the TST Main Loop near Bushkill Creek.

black bears (probably young adult brothers) on the Main Loop near Whittaker Road. I also saw a bear near Ben Hanna Swamp in 2024. Some of my hiking club colleagues have also reported bears in the aptly named Big Bear Swamp area at the far end of the Northeast Spur.

These predators should not present too much danger for hikers, but they definitely merit concern and wise behavior. Black bears tend to flee from humans long before they are seen, thanks to their remarkable sense of smell. A hiker should consider it great luck to even see one. Bears should not be provoked and definitely should not be fed, which increases the chances of their behavior changing abruptly from docile to aggressive. There is a chance of bears harassing untended campsites, though this should not be a serious concern for backpackers who take the necessary precautions.

The only truly dangerous animal in this area is the eastern timber rattlesnake. This snake prefers open areas for sunning and rocky outcrops for building dens. This species is venomous, but its bites are typically not fatal to healthy humans, with only a medium-strength temporary illness resulting for most people. (However, some people are highly allergic to the venom, leading to a more serious illness, and are probably unaware of their allergy until it is too late. Also, extra vigilance should be exercised for one's smaller hiking companions, such as dogs and young children.)

If bitten by a rattlesnake along the trail, do not panic. Return to your car quickly but in a levelheaded manner and seek medical attention as soon as possible. Contrary to popular opinion, rattlesnakes rarely attack humans—but rather defend themselves when provoked. In a telling reflection of human nature, upwards of 80% of snakebite victims anywhere in the world are bitten on their hands and arms after stupidly trying to pick up the snake. In the rare event that you encounter an eastern timber rattlesnake, retreat sensibly, leave it alone and consider yourself lucky to have seen this unique creature in its natural habitat.

A different problem arises from insects. Mosquitoes and similar pests are ubiquitous in the region, as are ticks. Lyme Disease has been reported in the area; and encounters with ticks (only a few of which actually carry the disease) are on the rise. High-quality insect repellent is crucial on Pennsylvania hiking trails during all seasons except the deepest parts of winter.

A Note on Hunting: Hunting is permitted in most of Delaware State Forest, including the areas traversed by the TST, and this particular area is popular with hunters from nearby states plus the locals. The author of this guide and the associated trail maintainers and Commonwealth personnel disavow all responsibility for the danger in which hikers may place themselves when hunters are present. Avoid hiking in state forest areas during the big game hunting seasons in the fall and early winter. If necessary, inquire with state forest personnel beforehand to learn which areas of the forest attract the most hunters. The Pennsylvania Game Commission also manages hunting seasons for many types of small game throughout the rest of the year, though these seasons present little risk for the hiker. Nevertheless, anyone hiking in areas known to be frequented by hunters is strongly advised to wear at least one prominent piece of "safety orange" clothing for visibility.

ACCESS AND LOGISTICS

ACCESS POINTS AND PARKING

As noted in the previous chapter, the Thunder Swamp Trail is easily reached from either I-80 or I-84, via PA 402. The TST Main Loop is roughly centered around that road and also encounters the paved Snow Hill Road. The Northeast Spur can be reached from the paved Bushkill Falls Road, which may be listed under other names on some maps but is easily recognizable as the high-use road that leads southeast from PA 402 to several Pocono tourist attractions.

To reach the TST from I-80, travel to the Stroudsburg area and use Exit 309, for US 209 northbound and PA 447 to Marshalls Creek. Ignore PA 447 and follow US 209 north for about 4.5 miles through the Stroudsburg suburbs to a junction with US 209 Business. Turn left (southbound) on that road and drive about 0.4 miles to the junction with PA 402 in the village of Marshalls Creek. Turn right (north) on PA 402. Beware that PA 402 almost immediately turns right again in front of a firehouse. Follow that route northbound; specific distances from Marshalls Creek are given below.

To reach the TST from I-84, travel to Exit 30, for PA 402 to Porters Lake and Blooming Grove. Follow PA 402 southbound; specific distances from I-84 are given below.

SOUTHERN TRAILHEAD (TST MAIN LOOP):

GPS LOCATION: N41° 08.866' W75° 04.812'

For the starting point of its description of the TST Main Loop, this guidebook uses the trailhead parking lot at the spot where the trail makes its southern crossing of PA 402. (The trail crosses that road again to the north, but there is no convenient parking at that spot.) The southern crossing features a very large recreational parking lot with two different driveways.

This sign for the Southern Trailhead on PA 402 is surprisingly easy to miss
if you are exceeding the speed limit.

From the south, follow PA 402 northbound for 8.1 miles from US 209 Business at Marshalls Creek. Start watching for the parking lot when you pass a signed boundary line into both Pike County and Delaware State Forest. The parking lot is on the right.

From the north, follow PA 402 southbound for 16.5 miles from I-84. From this direction the parking lot is on the left.

To reach the trail from this parking lot, use a very short access trail that departs from the north edge of the lot. You can also walk out to the main road via the northern driveway, and you will see the trail crossing the road a short distance to the right.

SNOW HILL ROAD (TST MAIN LOOP):

GPS LOCATION: N41° 09.881' W75° 07.200'

The TST Main Loop, at its 4.24 mi point, passes near this recreational parking lot on the narrow but paved Snow Hill Road.

From the south, follow PA 402 northbound for 10.2 miles from US 209 Business at Marshalls Creek to the intersection with Snow Hill Road. Turn left.

From the north, follow PA 402 southbound for 14.4 miles from I-84 to the intersection with Snow Hill Road. Turn right.

You have turned southwest onto Snow Hill Road. Follow this road for 2.3 miles to the forestry parking lot on the right. If the road reaches a low point at a bridge over a creek, you have missed the parking lot by about half a mile.

To reach the TST from this parking lot, walk back out to the road and turn right, downhill, for about 25 yards to a post sign. To follow the TST northbound, turn right at this sign. For southbound, stay on the road for an additional 15 yards then turn left.

RED ROCK RUN ROAD (TST MAIN LOOP):

GPS LOCATION: N41° 10.827' W75° 03.382'

The eastern section of the TST Main Loop is tough to reach by car. This parking spot on the unpaved Red Rock Run Road is viable for most vehicles but is not recommended in the winter.

From the south, follow PA 402 northbound for 10.5 miles from US 209 Business at Marshalls Creek, to the intersection with the unpaved Whittaker Farm Road. This is about 0.25 miles after Snow Hill Road. Turn right.

From the north, follow PA 402 southbound for 14.1 miles from I-84 to the intersection with the unpaved Whittaker Farm Road. Turn left. If you reach the intersection with Snow Hill Road, you have gone about 0.25 miles too far.

You have turned east on Whittaker Farm Road. At 0.8 miles, cross a long-distance powerline swath. At 1.0 miles, pass a "dead end" sign, after which the name changes to Red Rock Run Road (beware that some maps do not note this change, and other maps use the simpler Red Rock Road). Keep going past a few junctions until a fork in the road at 1.8 miles from PA 402. There is a small parking lot for 3-4 cars on the left. In this area the TST, if hiking southbound, has already been on the road behind you for a while, and then bears right onto Luke Road. You are at the 14.35 mi point on the TST Main Loop.

BUSHKILL FALLS ROAD (TST NORTHEAST SPUR):

GPS LOCATION: N41° 13.250' W75° 03.188'

The TST Northeast Spur passes near another very large recreational parking lot on the paved Bushkill Falls Road, to the southeast of PA 402. "Bushkill Falls Road" is the name used on the official maps from Delaware State Forest, though you may also see it labelled as Old Bushkill Road or simply Bushkill Road.

The parking lot is near the Northeast Spur's crossing of that road, at its 0.48 mi point. That point is also just 0.48 miles from the western end of the Northeast Spur, so this parking lot can also be used to reach the northern section of the TST Main Loop.

From the south, follow PA 402 northbound for 14.2 miles from US 209 Business at Marshalls Creek, to the intersection with Bushkill Falls Road. Turn right.

From the north, follow PA 402 southbound for 10.4 miles from I-84 to the intersection with Bushkill Falls Road. Turn left.

You have turned southeast on Bushkill Falls Road, following signs to several Pocono tourist attractions. Follow the road for 1.5 miles. Watch carefully for two different driveways on the right that lead through a wooded buffer to the recreational parking lot. You have just barely missed the lot if you reach the intersection of Flat Ridge Road on the left and Lake Minisink Road on the right.

As an alternative from the south, you can also reach this spot by following Bushkill Falls Road from US 209 at the village of Bushkill. Follow the road northbound, past the "Bushkill Falls" tourist attraction, for 10.2 miles. In this case the parking lot will be on the left, immediately after the intersection with Flat Ridge Road and Lake Minisink Road.

To reach the Northeast Spur from the parking lot, you will have to do a rather lengthy walk out the parking lot's southern driveway back to the road. Turn right and you will soon find the trail emerging from the woods just before the corner of Lake Minisink Road.

In a pinch: The only other viable parking spot near the TST system is an informal area in the village of Ludleyville, which is on PA 402 about 0.3 miles north of the TST's northern crossing of that road. Ludleyville is 12.6 miles north of Marshalls Creek and 12.0 miles south of I-84. In that village there is a grassy lane branching off from the northbound side of PA 402 that serves as a local day hike, and which leads southeast to the TST Main Loop at its 9.54 mi point. Informal parking may be available in the village, but this option is not generally recommended, if only for reasons of politeness.

Unlike most other Pennsylvania backpacking trails, the TST crosses very few roads of any kind beyond those described in this section.

MEASURING AND MAPPING TECHNIQUE

Your present author personally measured and mapped the Thunder Swamp Trail specifically for the first edition of this book in 2021. I used a Garmin Oregon 550 handheld GPS device and carefully corrected the resulting data to achieve maps and tables of measurements that were as close to reality as possible. In June 2024 I completed the trail again and made notes of a few minor changes that have been included in this new edition of the guidebook.

Please accept the figures in this book as "official" until the next volunteer comes along to measure the trail again. Admittedly, the accuracy of on-the-ground distance measurements via GPS has not yet been fully acknowledged by trail maintainers and veteran hikers, though most have accepted the accuracy of GPS mapping. A measuring wheel, which uses an odometer to measure feet or meters as the hiker pushes it along the trail, is remarkably accurate, even among multiple people who measure the same trail and compare their numbers. I once preferred to use such a device myself, but after getting into a jam when a measuring wheel broke in the middle of a project for one of my previous guidebooks, I switched to GPS measurements and learned how to carefully manage the data collected by my device with professional mapping software.

The maps included in this guide were created from the author's GPS data that was downloaded into professional mapping software. In the final pages of this book you will find small maps, plus a QR code and website address that can be used to access a more detailed online map, which was also created from the author's GPS data.

In addition, there is an excellent public use map denoting the Thunder Swamp Trail and several affiliated side trails, published by Delaware State Forest, while the system is also visible in the general map for the entire state forest. These are usually available at the information boards in the official State Forest parking lots and can be viewed online as well. At the time of writing, the most recent versions of these maps had been published in the late 2010s.

BACKPACKING TRIPS AND DAY HIKES

If you are a day hiker, do not be perturbed by the long distances of the Thunder Swamp Trail or any other backpacking trail. Hikers of all levels of skill and interest will find ways to enjoy a trail, from short afternoon jaunts to multi-day epics. All that matters is the planning.

At 18.28 miles, the TST Main Loop seems tailor-made for a two day/one night backpacking trip, and thanks to the lack of strenuous climbing, it can serve that purpose for beginners as well as experts. For a three-day/two-night trip measuring 31.67 miles, consider doing the west half of the Main Loop, completing the Northeast Spur in both directions back to the junction, and then finishing the east half of the Main Loop. The area's many yellow-blazed side trails could be utilized for creative backpacking loops as well.

Alas, there is a challenge in finding traditional camping spots (where you can pitch a tent and relax on the ground) due to the almost constantly rocky landscape. There are not very many such spots along the Main Loop, and even fewer along the Northeast Spur. Such spots are highlighted in the trail descriptions later in this book.

Since the TST is entirely within the borders of Delaware State Forest (plus Stillwater Natural Area for part of the Northeast Spur), primitive camping is allowed anywhere. Adventurous backpackers may be able to sniff out a spot but should prepare for a rough experience. Camping hammocks, which are becoming increasingly popular with backpackers, would certainly help on this trail because they can be hung from any two trees and do not require flat ground.

For day hikers of all levels of ability, the author of this book strongly recommends hikes of the out-and-back variety. Start at one of the more accessible parking spots, follow the trail for a certain distance, then turn around and return to your car. Not only can you tell your friends that you have completed that section of the trail twice, but this is a useful technique for piecing together a series of day hikes into a complete transit of a long-distance trail. Besides, hikers are often surprised by how much scenery they can miss by following a trail in only one direction. Just note that the trail descriptions in this book are one-way so if you are going in the opposite direction, left turns become right turns, uphill becomes downhill, and the like.

CAMPING

Hikers can camp in Delaware State Forest with supplies that they carry in themselves. The TST, notwithstanding the rocky landscape, is a good trail for practicing your overnight skills and assessing your ability to carry the heavy pack needed for tougher projects in the future. Consider taking the opportunity to park at a trailhead and walk a relatively short distance to a camping spot.

In Pennsylvania State Forest terminology, backcountry camping comes in two flavors: "car camping" (where you can park directly at a campsite) and "primitive camping" (on foot with a backpack). There are no car camping sites adjacent to the TST. Primitive camping is permitted anywhere in state forest lands, with some restrictions as listed below.

In Delaware State Forest, statewide camping rules apply. The Pennsylvania Department of Conservation and Natural Resources maintains rules and regulations for primitive camping on state forest lands. The Commonwealth utilizes camping permits, which are mostly used for recordkeeping and safety purposes, and are free of charge at the time of this writing. Also, at the time of writing, primitive backpackers are not required to apply for a camping permit except if any of the following conditions apply:

- An emergency point of contact is desired.
- You plan to stay at the same site for more than one night.
- A campfire is planned during the spring or fall fire seasons.
- You are "group camping" (more than 10 people).

This process is designed to control the damage that could result from large numbers of campers in sensitive areas. Note that camping permits are not issued to persons under 18. To apply for a camping permit, visit the DCNR website at www.dcnr.pa.gov. The site will direct you to navigate to the page for the applicable state forest district office where you will then find the necessary contact information and instructions.

Important Primitive Camping Rules: DCNR maintains many rules for primitive camping in the state forests. Some of these will seem like common sense to experienced outdoorspersons, but others are unique to Pennsylvania conditions. For the most up-to-date rules, see the official state document "Primitive Camping in State Forests and Parks" which can also be found at the DCNR website.

Backpackers in Pennsylvania should observe the following important rules, among others:

- Carry out all trash. Repeat: ALL trash.
- Choose a spot that does not require the clearing of vegetation.
- Stay at least 100 feet away from any flowing stream or open water source.
- Do not wash clothes, dishes, or campsite equipment directly in a stream or spring. Collect water in a container and do your washing away from the source, then dispose of the wastewater at least 200 feet from the source.
- Whenever possible, camp at least 25 feet from the trail, and preferably out of sight of the trail.
- Dispose of human waste by burying it in a hole at least 6 inches deep. Bring a camp trowel or small shovel for this purpose. Disposal sites should be at least 200 feet from water sources.
- Do not build a campfire during the dry seasons of spring and fall, or during other periods of abnormally high fire danger. At other times, small campfires are permitted. At previously unused campsites, construct a fire ring with nearby rocks to prevent the flames from spreading, and scatter the ring before leaving the site.
- Do not chop down live trees for firewood. Only use downed and dead wood near your campsite. Power saws are not permitted except with prior permission from the relevant state forest office.

Also, though it is not a state forest rule, beware of camping in or near the copses of rhododendron and mountain laurel that are common in Pennsylvania. These plants are flammable and may also provide cover for disagreeable animals.

Camping Locations Mentioned in This Guide: The author has made an effort to point out potential primitive camping spots along the trail, with selections being made for variety and the potential for pleasant backpacking experiences. However, not all these sites may completely comply with the above rules. Some areas within larger "sites" listed in this guide may not be 100 feet from a water source or 25 feet from the trail. The hiker will also notice many existing campsites created by previous backpackers, which may not comply with either of those strictures. The mention of such sites in this guide should not be considered an endorsement of the possibly illegal activities of previous backpackers.

Many of the possible campsites mentioned in this guide are near streams and springs, and to follow the state forest rules you would have to find a spot along the edge of such an area that is sufficiently removed from the water. All backpackers are strongly advised to follow the DCNR's primitive camping rules, which will ensure that future backpackers will not be deprived of the opportunity. Those using this guide will camp at the described spots at their own risk.

WATER

In this age of acid rain and bacterial pathogens, all water sources encountered in the wild should be viewed with suspicion. Giardia, a waterborne bacterium that causes the gastro-intestinal illness giardiasis, has been found in mountain streams throughout Pennsylvania. While experienced outdoorspersons might be comfortable drinking wild water, no hiking guide (including this one) will recommend doing so, and such actions will be taken at your own risk.

Water found along the trail should be treated with iodine capsules or submicron filters, which can be found at sports stores and outfitters. This is the recommended strategy for backpackers. The old-school method of purifying water by boiling it at a campfire is a tedious chore that is usually not worth the effort, even when boiling is actually achieved via a small wood fire. Day hikers should have little difficulty merely packing up the water they will need at home before embarking on their day trips.

Water Sources Listed in This Guide: Despite traversing a landscape speckled with swamps and wetlands, the Thunder Swamp Trail system encounters very few sources of water that can be reliably consumed by the hiker. This is because swamps and wetlands, by definition, are full of mud and plant life that are totally natural but create murky water. The same is true of the creeks in the area, most of which drain out of those same swamps.

As of 2024, the present author has completed the trails described in this guidebook multiple times during various seasons of the year, and has made an effort to describe the quality and seasonality of the water sources encountered along the trails. However, the user of this guide will consume any water found along the trail at his or her own risk. As a general rule, water found in swamps, muddy spots, seep springs, and backwaters along the sides of flowing streams should be avoided. Also, water from larger creeks should be avoided because wide waterways, by definition, have collected water from many tributaries and low-lying areas, increasing the chances of pollution. Also avoid taking water from streams that sport beaver dams, which alter natural filtration patterns.

This guide describes the suspected water quality (in the experienced hiker's estimation) of the many springs and small streams encountered along the trails discussed. These readings were *not* determined scientifically, should *not* be taken as any type of recommendation to drink the water, and should be considered as loose guidelines only. Water sources listed here as "poor" or "not suitable" should be avoided under all circumstances. Sources described as "questionable" could possibly be consumed by the desperate, or hikers with high-quality filters. Sources described as "acceptable" or "good" in this guide can be consumed by any hiker with store-bought filtering equipment.

A final note on water sources described in this guide: If you visit the trails during an especially dry period, beware that the flow and quality of springs and streams as described in this guide may be reduced. In fact, some may not even be flowing by the time you reach them. Wherever possible, efforts have been made to determine the quality of water sources during various seasons.

GUIDE TO THE THUNDER SWAMP TRAIL: MAIN LOOP

This chapter describes the Main Loop of the TST in the clockwise direction, starting from the main trailhead parking lot at the trail's southern crossing of PA 402. For driving directions to this and other parking spots, see the "Access and Logistics" chapter above. The description begins by walking westbound away from the highway.

Describing the trail in this fashion was an arbitrary decision by the author; descriptions of the trail in other publications might be in the opposite direction. You are free to hike in any direction you want.

MI	KM	DESCRIPTION
0.00	0.00	The main Thunder Swamp Trail loop begins just north of the trailhead parking lot on PA 402. To reach this point, you can simply walk north on the highway a short distance from the parking lot's northern driveway, or you can use a very brief access trail out of the northern edge of the parking lot and then turn left on the main trail. To follow the loop clockwise as described in this guide, cross the highway and head west; be vigilant because the speed limit is 45 MPH, and of course everyone goes faster than that.
0.03	0.05	Trail register; please sign in. The TST begins a long, mild descent through a very rocky area. In this area, as of 2025 there are plans to build a short side trail that will head off to the left toward the nearby Delaware State Forest office building.

MI	KM	DESCRIPTION
0.47	0.76	Begin a steeper descent into a hollow.
0.56	0.91	Walk through a low area where an intermittent run disappears under hemlock roots and reappears several times. Acceptable water quality a short distance downstream.
0.73	1.18	After a moderate climb, scramble up some rock ledges and bear left through a high meadow. It appears that there may have once been a homestead or other building here.
0.96	1.55	Turn left alongside the large Ben Hanna Swamp.
0.99	1.59	Cross a deep run that drains out of the swamp. This will be a tricky crossing on rocks or fallen logs. Poor water quality. Next, there is a nice view of the swamp to your right. Note the clutch of tall dead trees in the foreground. These may have once been high and dry; but later ended up under water and died when the swamp expanded. This is a sign of beaver activity.

Ben Hanna Swamp, the first of several large swamps visible from the TST.

MI	KM	DESCRIPTION
1.37	2.21	Enter a vast sea of ferns. This may look like a pleasantly green forest, but you will notice very few young trees. This is an indicator of deer overpopulation in the general area because the deer eat baby trees as soon as they pop out of the ground. Since deer usually do not eat ferns, the result is heavy fern undergrowth with few new trees to replace the older ones as they die off. This is a serious challenge for forest management throughout Pennsylvania.
1.56	2.51	Curve broadly to the right along the edge of a hollow. I saw a bear in this area while researching this guidebook in spring 2024.
1.88	3.02	Curve left and begin a moderately steep descent toward the hollow.
2.17	3.49	Continue descending through a wet and rocky area where some seep springs have commandeered the trail.
2.37	3.81	Reach a relatively flat area where you begin to see the wide and robust Bushkill Creek through the trees. Between here and the creek there are some possible campsites, though the ground is uneven.
2.41	3.89	Turn right along the high embankment above the creek. There is a great camping spot downhill to the left.
2.50	4.03	Scramble down to a rock outcropping above the creek. This is a nice spot for a break. The TST immediately climbs back up the embankment.
2.56	4.13	The trail walks along the creek for a while then curves inland. Bushkill Creek is a tempting spot for a swim on a hot day but beware of a very strong current. Also, taking water from the creek is not recommended because it has already collected several tributaries of questionable quality.
2.75	4.44	Walk through a rare natural campsite. It appears that this is a popular spot, and rightfully so because there are very few such sites along the TST. This is your last close encounter with Bushkill Creek. Next, hop over two intermittent runs with poor water quality.

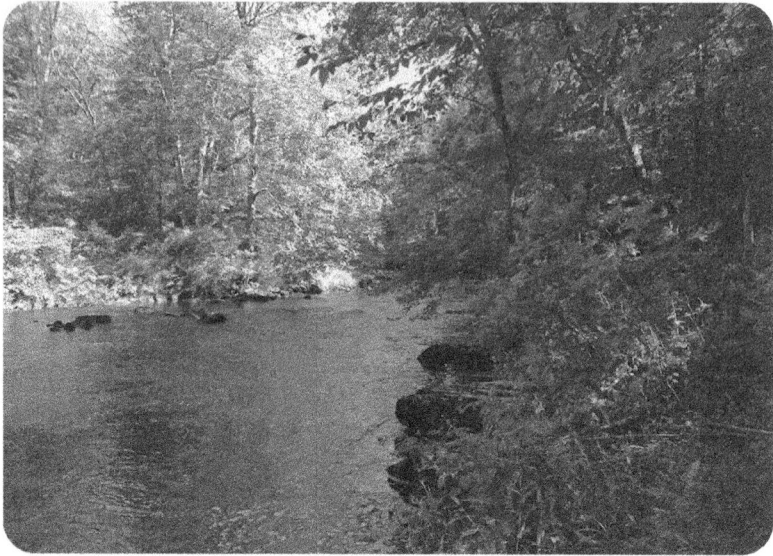

Bushkill Creek as seen from the trail.

MI	KM	DESCRIPTION
2.80	4.50	Turn right into a brushy area, then briefly walk up the rocky bed of an intermittent run.
2.83	4.55	Hop over two channels of an incoming stream. These may have acceptable water quality in season.
3.01	4.85	Cross a usually dry run. Begin a long, mild climb away from the Bushkill Creek bottomlands.
3.50	5.64	You have reached the top of the plateau. Continue across a generally flat landscape.
3.58	5.77	With an open meadow to the right, cross an unmarked trail at an angle and continue ahead.
3.68	5.92	Turn sharply right in an otherwise nondescript area.
3.93	6.32	Just after a rough, rocky stretch, cross two channels of an intermittent run. Next, slog through a few mudpits.
4.01	6.46	Turn left on a forestry maintenance road. Follow the road briefly for about 20 yards, and then turn right, back into the woods.

MI	KM	DESCRIPTION
4.20	6.77	Trail register; please sign in.
4.23	6.81	Turn right briefly on the paved Snow Hill Road and head uphill for about 15 yards.
4.24	6.83	Turn left at a post sign and head northwest into the woods. The Snow Hill Road parking lot is a short distance further up the road.
4.26	6.86	Another trail register; please sign in again. The Thunder Swamp Trail network tends to have trail registers on both sides of a notable road crossing. This may seem repetitive to through-hikers, but some hikers make use of shorter segments. Sign all of them because this provides maximum information for forestry officials about who is using the trail and for what types of hikes.
		The TST continues ahead northbound. For about the next 1.2 miles, prepare for a journey that is even rockier than usual.
4.89	7.87	With the swampy Spruce Run just to the left (questionable water quality), turn abruptly right and head away from the run for a while.
5.05	8.14	Cross an intermittent stream (not suitable for drinking).
5.09	8.19	Cross a footbridge over Spruce Run, which drains out of a large swamp to the right.
5.43	8.74	Begin a moderate climb up a series of low ridgelines. Near the top of the climb, there is a tricky spot where you briefly follow a usually dry streambed and then bear right. Watch the blazes carefully. The trail then levels off in a high area and finally becomes less rocky.
5.75	9.25	Continue ahead at a junction with a yellow-blazed trail. (To the left, the yellow-blazed trail leads about half a mile to Pennel Run Natural Area, which was damaged by a forest fire in the late 2010s. After allowing the ecosystem some time to recover, as of 2025 forestry officials plan to build a new loop trail through the natural area.)

MI	KM	DESCRIPTION
6.00	9.67	Cross two footbridges that are separated by a brief stretch of rocky ground. These bridges go over two branches of Spruce Run, out of yet another swamp to the left. The two streams are usually murky or intermittent, so drinking the water is not advised. After the second bridge, turn left and climb through an area that is prone to heavy overgrowth. Some views of the swamp open up to your left.
6.17	9.93	Cross an upper tributary of Spruce Run on rocks (questionable water quality).
6.21	10.00	Pass through a rare camping spot in a flat grassy area, then cross another branch of Spruce Run on rocks (questionable water quality).
6.38	10.28	After a brief descent, turn abruptly right and proceed through a low, rocky area.
6.43	10.36	Pass through a clutch of large boulders.
6.69	10.78	Pass by the remains of an old rock wall that has been disrupted by a tree.
6.98	11.24	The trail turns right and climbs briefly to a shrubbery-choked hilltop.
7.25	11.67	After a barely noticeable rise in the landscape, note the abrupt change in the nature of the forest, with young and thin hardwoods suddenly becoming dominant.
7.41	11.94	After another brief rise, enter yet another type of forest ecosystem dominated by mature hardwoods.
7.81	12.58	Cross an old forestry road at an angle and continue ahead. (This lane is labelled as Spruce Run Trail on some maps. To the left, it leads 1.3 miles to Beaver Run Road.)
8.30	13.37	The trail is just below the top of a ridgeline, with a long and narrow valley falling away to the right. Most of that valley is occupied by the aptly named Big Swamp, though you cannot see that swamp from here.

MI	KM	DESCRIPTION
8.54	13.76	Turn right, cross a usually dry run, then turn right again.
8.66	13.94	Curve to the left in a hemlock grove.
9.38	15.11	Pass a junction with a yellow-blazed trail, which heads left to Beaver Run Road. After the junction, the TST heads across a wide powerline swath. There are a few turns as you traverse the swath, which is tricky because there are no trees on which to paint blazes. Watch the footway carefully.
9.42	15.17	At the far side of the powerline swath, turn right into the trees, after which PA 402 is a short distance to your left.
9.45	15.22	Trail register; please sign in. Next is a tricky wet area caused by runoff from the road.
9.49	15.29	Climb up to PA 402, hop over the guardrail, and cross the highway very carefully. This is a high-speed stretch of road with limited sight distance for drivers. Jog a short distance down the road to the left, then turn back into the woods just before the start of another guardrail.
		There is no convenient parking within sight of this crossing. Ludleyville is about 0.3 miles down the road to the left (north). Some informal parking is available near the corner of an old grassy track off the north-bound lane of PA 402. That track serves as a local day hike and leads south to the TST; meeting the main trail at the junction described in the next entry below. Also note that Ludleyville is just a small hamlet of private homes and there are no retail or emergency services for hikers.
9.54	15.37	Reach an intersection of three different grassy lanes. Please sign in again at the trail register. The lane to the left goes back to PA 402 in Ludleyville, as described in the entry above. The TST continues on the grassy lane that continues straight ahead (northeast) and away from PA 402.

MI	KM	DESCRIPTION
9.58	15.43	Walk around a vehicle gate and continue on an easy forestry road. If you are circuit-hiking the Thunder Swamp Trail as described in this guide, use this area to make up a bit of the time you lost during the past nine rocky miles. (Never fear, the rocks will be back soon enough.)
9.73	15.67	Bear right at a fork in the lane. Ahead, the lane you're following gets narrower but remains easy.
10.16	16.36	Pass a small campsite with a swampy section of Saw Creek off to the right. Be skeptical of water quality in the creek. Next, the old grassy lane fizzles out and you continue on a narrow footpath over a low hill. This is a generally favorable area for camping, with some open and flat areas within sight, though you might have to do a little exploring off the trail.
10.26	16.53	Enter a fairly open valley where you will see bountiful wildflowers. The sluggish and irregular Saw Creek is still to the right.
10.40	16.75	Reach one of the more unique features to be found on the TST, or any hiking trail in Pennsylvania, for that matter. First, note the overgrown old quarry to the left, from where rocks were mined to build your next item of interest. The TST turns right, crosses a short footbridge, and then walks across the top of a delightfully weathered old stone dam that was built across Saw Creek. The exact origins of this dam seem to be lost in the mists of time, but off the trail in this area there is some evidence of old milling operations, which were probably affiliated with the dam and its artificial lake. The lake was probably more robust at the time, and it currently shows signs of filling up with mud and vegetation, which is not a surprise in such a swampy area.
10.43	16.79	Cross another short footbridge, which goes over an outflow break in the old stone dam. Continue walking across the top of the dam. At the end, jump up a rock ledge to higher ground and turn left.

The old stone dam, weathered and colonized
by plant life.

MI	KM	DESCRIPTION
10.46	16.85	Turn right at the junction with a yellow-blazed trail. Next, pass through a soggy area that could be a challenge during rainy periods.
10.49	16.89	Go straight ahead at another trail junction, this time with the yellow-blazed Thunder Swamp Spur Trail which heads to the right. After the junction, begin a brief climb up a minor ridgeline. At the top of the climb, the TST continues in a fairly straight line to east-northeast, rising gently to moderately for the next 0.38 mi (0.61 km). (Do not confuse the trail at this last junction with the main Thunder Swamp Trail with orange blazes that you are following. The spur trail loops back around

MI	KM	DESCRIPTION
(cont.)		to Ludleyville. Meanwhile, the carsonite post features numbers that correspond to points on some recreational maps published by Delaware State Forest.)
10.87	17.50	Climb steeply but briefly through a boulder field, after which the trail levels off in a young forest.
11.07	17.82	Reach the most important junction in the Thunder Swamp Trail system. The Northeast Spur, also orange-blazed, turns left here and heads toward Painter Swamp. (See the separate chapter on the Northeast Spur later in this book). The main TST loop turns right at this junction and heads to the south.
11.11	17.88	Pass through a small meadow that sits on top of a short cliff, with lots of shattered shale underfoot. There is a dim view of Lake Minisink through the trees to the left.
11.21	18.05	Turn left for a steep plunge off a rocky ridgeline. Watch for this turn carefully because a different unblazed trail goes straight ahead.
11.34	18.25	After reaching high ground again, there is another partial view of Lake Minisink through the trees to the left.
11.42	18.40	Cross a muddy run that is usually dry or intermittent; not suitable for drinking most of the year.
11.88	19.13	Diagonal climb up a low ridgeline.
12.22	19.67	Cross the paved but narrow Whittaker Road (mostly used by ATVs), then continue straight ahead.
12.38	19.94	Cross a small run (questionable water quality). The trail next climbs moderately to another hilltop area. In a previous visit, the author saw two black bears, probably young adult brothers, in this area.
12.72	20.48	Pass a clutch of algae-covered boulders.
12.92	20.81	Turn left onto an old road grade.

MI	KM	DESCRIPTION
12.96	20.86	In a grassy meadow, turn right on to another old lane. Follow this one uphill for about 20 yards then turn right again onto a narrower footpath. Watch blazes carefully.
13.29	21.40	Cross a muddy run; not suitable for drinking most of the year. Continue ahead uneventfully over a pretty rocky landscape that trends gradually downhill for the next 0.85 mi (1.37 km).
14.14	22.77	Turn left, uphill, on Red Rock Run Road (also known as Whittaker Farm Road or the simpler Red Rock Road on some maps). At the time of writing, the trail sign here misleadingly points straight ahead; turn left onto the road instead. The arrows on the other side of the sign are the wrong color too. Also, ignore the plastic signs of various colors in this area, which are meant for snowmobilers. Turn left on the road and continue to follow the basic orange blazes of the TST. Stay on the road for the next 0.21 mi (0.34 km).
14.30	23.03	Possible parking spot on the left at the junction with an old maintenance road. Never park in front of any gates.
14.35	23.11	Reach a fork in the road with a small unpaved parking lot (3-4 cars) on the left. For directions on driving to this point, see the "Access and Logistics" chapter earlier in this book. At the fork in the road, the TST bears right onto the gated Luke Road, which you will follow for the next 1.24 mi. (1.99 km). For much of your journey on Luke Road, recent logging zones are visible to the left.
15.59	25.10	The vehicular segment of Luke Road finally ends at a large clearing that was recently formed by loggers. Continue straight ahead on a narrower grassy lane, descending. Watch blazes carefully.

MI	KM	DESCRIPTION
15.61	25.14	Turn right into the woods at a post sign. After the turn, you will be able to hear Red Rock Run to your left.
15.81	25.46	Traverse a very rocky and jumbled area with Red Rock Run just to your left. There are a couple of rare camping spots here and there on both sides of the creek. Despite its dark coloration, the water in the creek is of acceptable quality. The coloration is natural and is provided by the unique plants of the region. This is a common characteristic of many of the streams encountered along the Thunder Swamp Trail.
16.21	26.11	Reach a nice spot for a break as Red Rock Run splits into multiple channels with small islands and waterfalls. Next, the trail turns right and heads away from the creek for the time being.
16.59	26.72	Bear left and pass under a long-distance powerline swath (the same powerline encountered about seven miles ago in the Ludleyville area). Watch carefully for a post with an orange blaze on the far side, and beware of tricky footway. The TST reenters the woods, still parallel to Red Rock Run.
16.73	26.94	Traverse a pretty area alongside the creek, with some viable but cramped camping spots here and there.
16.78	27.02	Find another rare camping spot just above an unusual waterfall in Red Rock Run, which is one of the most scenic features to be found on the Thunder Swamp Trail. You can scramble down to a large boulder for a nice view. Known variously as a "fan waterfall" or "slide waterfall," this type of fall serves as a sort of diagonal riffle over a monolithic layer of bedrock, which is rare in Pennsylvania.
16.85	27.13	Reach the creekside again along a stretch with several multi-step waterfalls.

The slide waterfall on Red Rock Run.

MI	KM	DESCRIPTION
16.99	27.36	Cross the high footbridge over the deep and swift Saw Creek, which suddenly appears from the right. The TST also encountered Saw Creek at the old stone dam along the northern section of the Main Loop. Here, the confluence of Saw Creek and Red Rock Run is visible just to the left, downstream.
		At the time of writing, this crossing featured a bridge that was built by Keystone Trails Association volunteers in 1986. The bridge is becoming wobbly and uneven, and in 2025, personnel at Delaware State Forest decided to replace this bridge for safety purposes. The completion date of the new bridge is unknown as of this writing in mid-2025. Also note that the new bridge may not be in the same location as the old one, so the route of the trail may alter slightly.
		After the bridge, turn right and follow Saw Creek upstream. Avoid taking water from the creek because it has collected many questionable tributaries and has been dammed several times by creatures great and small.
17.03	27.42	Turn left and climb briefly.

The view downstream from the Saw Creek bridge.

MI	KM	DESCRIPTION
17.04	27.44	Turn right at a junction with Tim's Swamp Trail. (That trail follows Saw Creek downstream for a while then heads west to PA 402.)
17.08	27.50	You are still parallel to Saw Creek but now about 30 feet above it. Pass through a nice but overused natural campsite.
17.12	27.56	Cross a small run on rocks; poor water quality. Next, the trail curves broadly to the left and away from Saw Creek.
17.23	27.74	Bear left on an old road grade that heads south.
17.26	27.80	Note that the TST has made a U-turn as you again meet the murky stream that you crossed on rocks a few minutes ago. Do the same this time.
17.49	28.16	The old road grade is now climbing moderately and shows signs of being washed out several times during periods of high water. On the way up, cross another small run on rocks; questionable water quality.

MI	KM	DESCRIPTION
17.52	28.21	Reach a junction with a yellow-blazed trail that goes straight ahead. (That trail is an extension of Tim's Swamp Road and heads to PA 402 on a route roughly parallel to the TST.) The TST turns right at this junction and climbs briefly.
17.55	28.27	At the top of the climb, turn right at the edge of a large swamp. Next, cross four different channels of the outlet stream (questionable water quality), which later unite into the single channel that you crossed a few minutes ago before the trail junction. Continue ahead with the swamp to your left. You are likely to hear bullfrogs in the swamp. Over the course of several visits, I have also heard various birds of prey, wild turkeys, and even owls in this area. After the swamp, embark on a long and mildly strenuous climb through open, high-altitude woods.
17.97	28.94	You have reached the plateau-top, but the footway becomes much rockier. In this area you begin to hear traffic on PA 402.

This swamp is full of life that is tough to see but easy to hear.

MI	KM	DESCRIPTION
18.23	29.36	Trail register; please sign in.
18.26	29.40	Reach a trail junction. The TST trailhead parking area on PA 402 is just ahead. Officially, the TST turns right here and heads out to the highway, parallel to the parking lot's northern driveway.
18.28	29.43	Reach PA 402. This is the end of the main loop of the Thunder Swamp Trail. Cross the road to do it again!

GUIDE TO THE THUNDER SWAMP TRAIL: NORTHEAST SPUR

This chapter describes the Northeast Spur of the TST, starting from its origin at the 11.07 mi point on the Main Loop. The Northeast Spur is described as heading to the northeast to the beginning of the Big Bear Swamp Loop, with that loop described in one direction (clockwise). This chapter then guides your return trip as you follow the Northeast Spur again in the opposite direction back to its starting point. The total distance of 13.39 miles includes both walks on the two-way segment of the Northeast Spur.

MI	KM	DESCRIPTION
0.00	0.00	From the junction at the 11.07 mi point on the TST Main Loop, the Northeast Spur (also orange-blazed) initially heads north, following the sign to Painter Swamp. The trail descends moderately through a rocky zone.
0.16	0.25	Just after a signpost, reach a small clearing next to a gravel road that currently serves as the Burnt Mills Trail for ATVs. Ahead, avoid joining the road and stay on the orange-blazed footpath that parallels the road just to the right. Also, do not turn sharply right onto the adjoining snowmobile trail. Watch the TST blazes carefully.
0.34	0.54	Reach the gravel road again. This time, turn right (east), walk about 15 yards, then turn right again back into the woods. You have missed the turn off the road if you reach a vehicle gate. Meanwhile, the road ahead leads to the parking area on Bushkill Falls Road.

MI	KM	DESCRIPTION
0.39	0.63	Cross a powerline swath. To the left, this swath provides another shortcut to the parking area, though some bushwhacking will be required.
0.47	0.76	Trail register; please sign in.
0.48	0.77	Emerge at a four-way intersection of the paved Bushkill Falls Road, Lake Minisink Road (behind), and Flat Ridge Road (ahead). The driveway to the recreational parking area is just down the paved road to the left. Cross the intersection carefully at an angle. You will have to go a brief distance up Bushkill Falls Road to the right, then continue your hike eastbound on a footpath to the right of Flat Ridge Road.
0.53	0.85	Trail register; please sign in. Even though you just saw a different trail register a few minutes ago, it helps to sign all that you encounter so forest managers have maximum information on how many people use the trail.
0.59	0.96	Cross an old jeep road.
0.62	1.00	Climb up a minor ridgeline and curve left into a flat area, which looks like it might be an old homestead. Continue ahead uneventfully for the next 0.50 mi (0.80 km).
1.12	1.80	The trail scrambles down a minor ridgeline and then curves broadly to the left (northeast).
1.60	2.58	Turn sharply left in a generally nondescript area. Note the rock ledge to the left of the trail.
1.86	3.00	Make a U-turn to the left in an old meadow that is likely to be overgrown with ferns.
1.89	3.04	Curve right at the bottom of another low ridgeline.
2.00	3.23	Turn right on a gated maintenance road. Stay on this road for the next 0.34 mi (0.54 km).
2.10	3.38	Continue ahead through a triangle intersection with a driveway that comes up out of a quarry on the left.

MI	KM	DESCRIPTION
2.25	3.63	Bear left at an intersection with an old grassy lane.
2.34	3.77	Turn left off the road and onto a footpath. There should be a post sign at this turn but watch for the turn carefully regardless.
2.54	4.09	Pass through a grove of large old hemlocks. Due to the rocky terrain, these trees are unable to send their roots deep into the ground, so they spread out laterally and intertwine, creating a strange lumpy landscape with a fair number of ankle-busting holes between roots and rocks.
2.57	4.14	Reach the murky Painter Swamp Creek (questionable water quality), which drains out of the large swamp of the same name off to the left. Do not cross the creek straight ahead; instead turn left and walk up a rocky section of the streambed. The water is usually well beneath these rocks. Then bear right back into the woods. Next, bear right again in a small rocky clearing. Watch the blazes carefully in this area. The swamp is to your left for a short time, and then you continue northbound across a generally flat but rocky landscape for the next 0.74 mi (1.18 km).
3.31	5.32	Turn right at a junction with the yellow-blazed Painter Swamp Trail. Of interest: "Painter" is an old-time Pennsylvania slang term for a panther or mountain lion. (To the left, that trail goes about 0.25 miles to its namesake swamp, follows a loop around a small lake associated with the swamp complex, and ultimately leads to a parking area on Flat Ridge Road.)
3.32	5.35	Turn right again at a junction with an unblazed trail. (When you come back in the opposite direction later, this turn is easy to miss. See the 10.07 mi entry below.)
3.74	6.03	Trail register; please sign in.

MI	KM	DESCRIPTION
3.77	6.07	Turn right briefly on the gated Coon Swamp Road, which also serves as a portion of the yellow-blazed Coon Swamp Trail. Then turn left back into the woods. The Northeast Spur continues eastbound into a corner of Stillwater Natural Area and will remain in this district for most of the rest of its distance until you return to this point.
3.79	6.11	Another trail register; please sign in again. Regarding the repetitive trail registers, note that there are many trails in this area and the TST Northeast Spur can be used for creative loops, and this is also of interest to forest managers.
4.19	6.75	Turn right at a junction with a yellow-blazed trail that heads into the northern reaches of Stillwater Natural Area.
4.23	6.82	Plunge steeply but briefly down one of the more prominent ridgelines to be found in the TST network.

The Northeast Spur's bridge over Little Bushkill Creek.

MI	KM	DESCRIPTION
4.34	7.00	Cross the high footbridge over Little Bushkill Creek. There are some nice camping spots on the far side. Be suspicious of water quality in the creek. Shortly after the bridge, the trail joins an easy old road grade, which you will follow for the next 0.39 mi (0.62 km).
		Of interest: About eight miles south of here, Little Bushkill Creek forms the "Bushkill Falls" tourist attraction near US 209.
4.70	7.56	Still on the old road grade, pass through an impressive jungle of mountain laurel, which tends to encroach upon the trail.
4.73	7.62	Just before reaching an unnamed run, turn left and head upstream.
4.76	7.67	Turn right and cross the run on rocks. (Questionable water quality.) The forest in this area is fairly open and there are some possibilities for camping, though the ground is often lumpy. Next, begin a moderate climb back to the height of land.
4.97	8.01	Reach the junction with the Big Bear Swamp Loop, which serves as the turnaround for the TST Northeast Spur. The loop follows an old jeep road in this immediate area. The Northeast Spur turns here, goes around the loop, and returns to this point. At the time of writing, a sign at this junction says the loop is 5 miles around, but in reality, it is only 3.45 miles (5.55 km). To complete the loop clockwise as described in this guide, turn left here.
		If you can allow the author a moment of brutal honesty, the Big Bear Swamp Loop is a disappointment. You will travel in a large circle around the swamp of that name but will not see the actual swamp one single time. Instead, the loop simply rambles through typical woods without much variety in the scenery. Unless you are passionate about completing the entire TST system, you could consider ditching the loop and turning around here; if so, skip to the 8.42 mi entry below.

MI	KM	DESCRIPTION
5.33	8.58	Turn right off the old road and onto a narrow footpath.
5.64	9.08	Pass through a dry but intriguing camping area on top of a flat slab of bedrock that spreads out for about a quarter of an acre.
5.68	9.14	Step down off the giant rock slab and turn sharply right.
5.88	9.46	Pass through a low brushy zone that could be soggy during rainy periods.
5.90	9.50	Bear right and head up a hillside diagonally.
6.28	10.11	Through the trees to the right, you can see some soggy areas that are the closest you will get to the vast Big Bear Swamp, which you are currently walking around at a distance. Not unlike Captain Cook, who in the 1770s circumnavigated Antarctica, never seeing it once. You may consider some off-trail exploration to see the swamp; but note that there are bears in the area, and it is easy to get turned around in the tricky wetland environment.
6.38	10.28	Reach a generally wet area that will cause a serious challenge during rainy periods and remains tricky for most of the year. You may have to jump across various logs, rocks, and hummocks to the far side. This is a small wetland that flows into Big Bear Swamp to the right. The trail then rises briefly to higher ground. Continue ahead uneventfully, south then west, for the next 1.53 mi (2.46 km).
7.91	12.74	After an especially monotonous journey since the last point of interest, turn right on an old road grade. Stay on this lane for the next 0.51 mi (0.82 km).
8.30	13.36	Cross the robust Big Bear Run, which drains out of its namesake swamp and heads toward Little Bushkill Creek. Adequate water quality. For most of the year you should be able to hop across on rocks. Shortly after the crossing, bear right at a junction of grassy lanes.

MI	KM	DESCRIPTION
8.42	13.56	Reach the end of the Big Bear Swamp Loop, returning to the junction you departed from 3.45 miles ago (see the 4.97 mi entry above). Turn left to begin the return trip back to the start of the Northeast Spur. The trail description that continues below is a simplified version of the segment that you have already followed in the opposite direction.
9.05	14.57	Bridge over Little Bushkill Creek.
9.20	14.81	Turn left at the junction with the trail that heads into the northern reaches of Stillwater Natural Area.
9.62	15.49	Turn right briefly on Coon Swamp Road then turn left back into the woods.
10.07	16.22	Watch carefully for a surprise left turn (see the 3.32 mi entry above) from one narrow footpath to another. You have missed this turn if you come within view of a hunting camp.
10.82	17.42	Cross Painter Swamp Creek by briefly walking down its rocky bed.
11.05	17.79	Turn right on the forest maintenance road that passes the quarry.
11.39	18.34	Turn left off the road and onto a footpath.
12.91	20.79	Reach the four-way intersection of Bushkill Falls Road, Flat Ridge Road (behind), and Lake Minisink Road (ahead). You will have to jog right on the paved road. The driveway to the recreational parking lot is down that road to the right. The trail continues southwest into the woods to the right of Lake Minisink Road.
13.39	21.56	Reach the western end of the Northeast Spur at the 11.07 mi point on the Thunder Swamp Trail Main Loop. From this junction, the Main Loop goes right (counter-clockwise toward Ludleyville) or straight ahead (clockwise toward Red Rock Run Road).

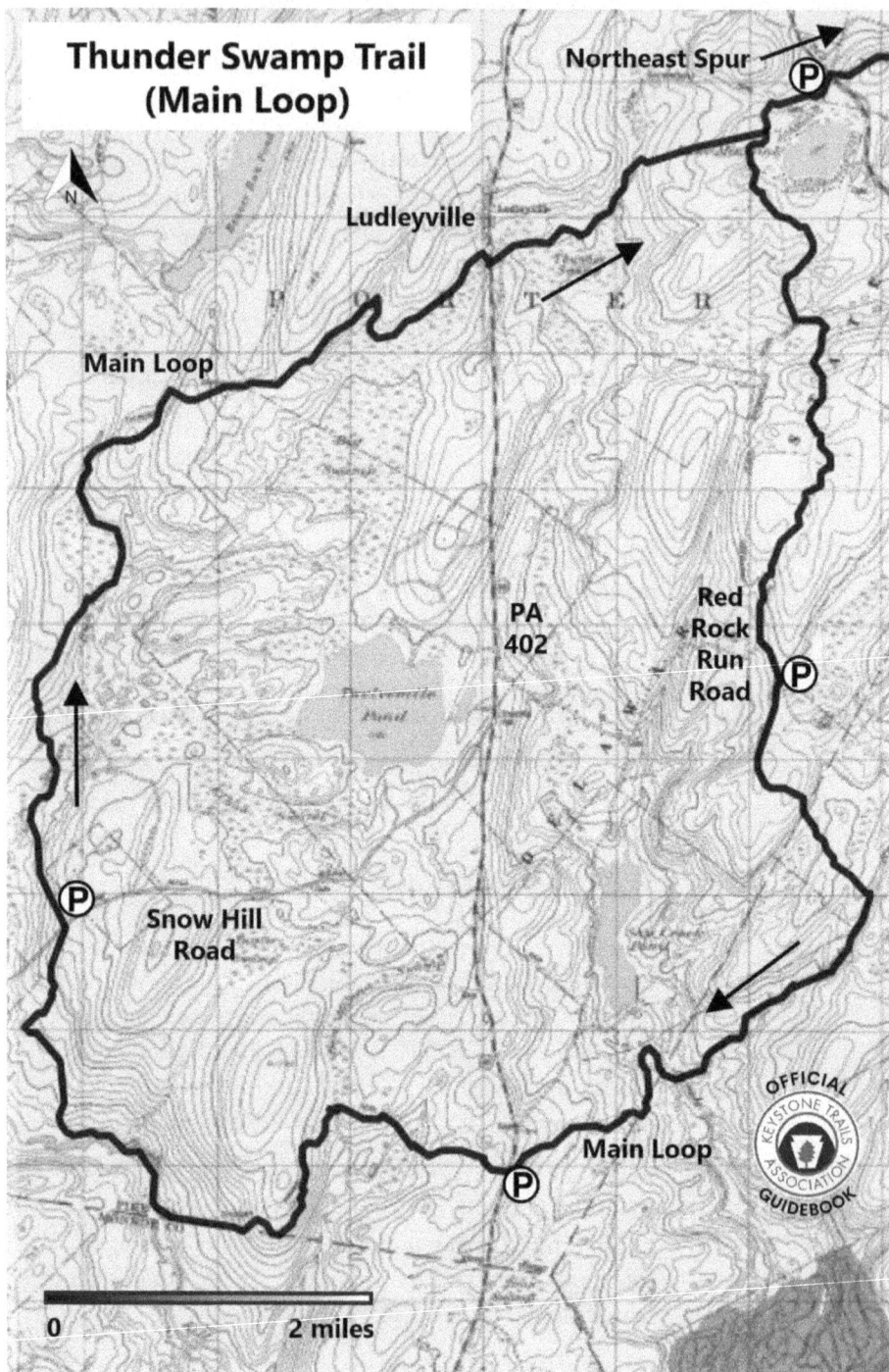

Thunder Swamp Trail
(Main Loop)

Northeast Spur

N

Ludleyville

Main Loop

PA 402

Red Rock Run Road

Snow Hill Road

Main Loop

OFFICIAL KEYSTONE TRAILS ASSOCIATION GUIDEBOOK

0   2 miles

Thunder Swamp Trail
(Northeast Spur)

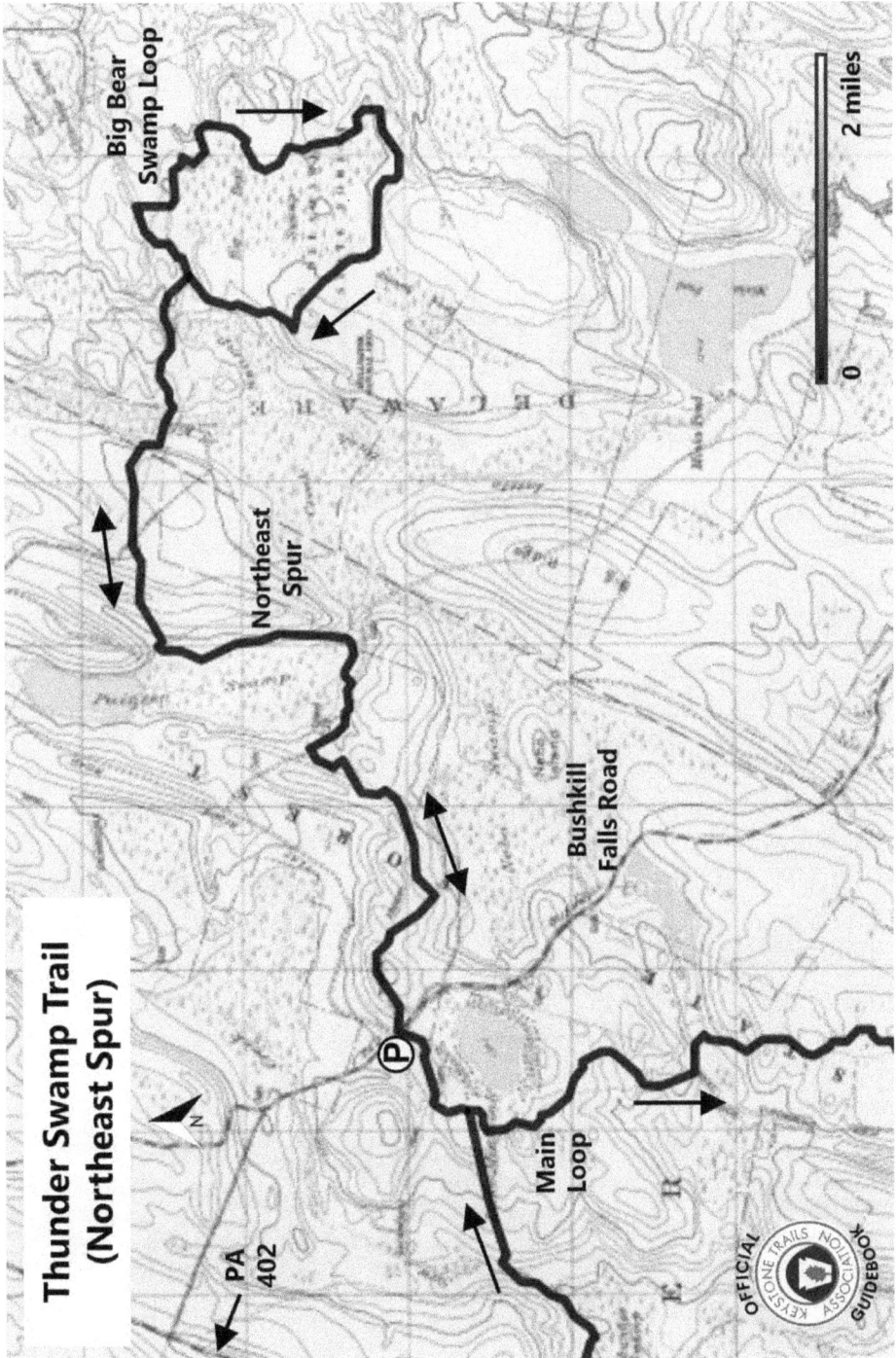

Big Bear
Swamp Loop

Northeast
Spur

Bushkill
Falls Road

Main
Loop

PA
402

N

2 miles

0

OFFICIAL KEYSTONE TRAILS ASSOCIATION GUIDEBOOK

For a larger online map of the Thunder Swamp Trail,
visit Keystone Trails Association at:

www.kta-hike.org/maps

or scan here:

These maps illustrate GPS data collected by the author. The online map is courtesy of CalTopo. The printed map on the previous two pages was created with GPS Visualizer, founded and operated by Adam Schneider, with USGS (United States Geologic Survey) maps as the backgrounds. All maps and data are verified for accuracy by the author and Keystone Trails Association.

ABOUT THE AUTHOR

Ben Cramer has hiked more than 6,000 miles on Pennsylvania's hiking trails and has completed many of the state's long-distance backpacking trails multiple times. He is a longtime member of Keystone Trails Association and was a member of its board of directors from 2018 to 2023. He is also a member of several Pennsylvania conservation groups and hiking clubs, and he was formerly an executive committee member for Sierra Club at both the local and state levels.

Cramer is the author of seven guidebooks for Pennsylvania backpacking trails, including one previous edition for the Thunder Swamp Trail. With one exception, none of those long-distance trails had dedicated guidebooks previously. Cramer was also the editor of *Pennsylvania Hiking Trails* (13th edition, 2008). For several years he wrote regularly on outdoor adventure and environmental issues for *The Centre Daily Times* and for a variety of Pennsylvania volunteer publications.

Under his professional name Benjamin W. Cramer, he is the author of the book *Freedom of Environmental Information* (2011). He is a longtime resident of State College, PA and teaches for the Donald P. Bellisario College of Communications at Penn State University, where one of his research specialties is the environmental impacts of modern telecommunications services.

www.ingramcontent.com/pod-product-compliance
Lightning Source LLC
Chambersburg PA
CBHW022342040426
42449CB00006B/681